Quarter-Note Slash

1 beat
Hold strum for one beat.

Treble Clef

$\frac{4}{4}$

$$\frac{4}{4}$$

Time Signature:
Four-Four Time

4 equal beats in every measure.

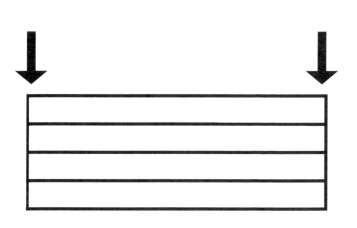

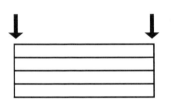

Bar Lines

Divide the staff into equal parts.

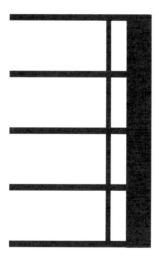

Double Bar Line

Shows the music is finished.

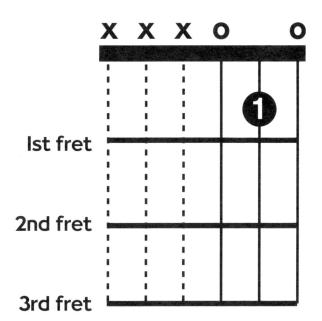

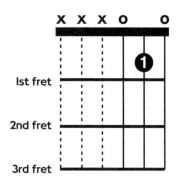

Three-String C Chord

Quarter Rest

1 beat

Be silent for one beat.

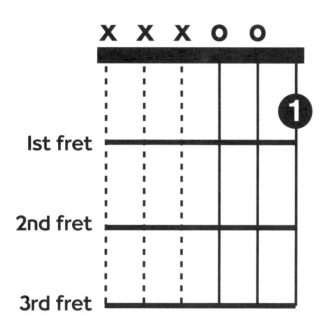

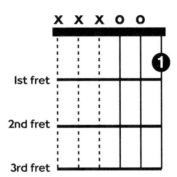

Three-String G⁷ Chord

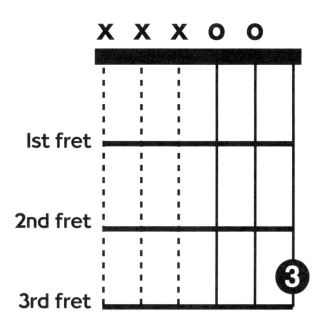

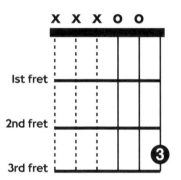

Three-String G Chord

Repeat Sign

Repeat from the beginning.

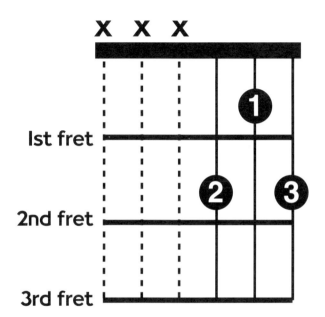

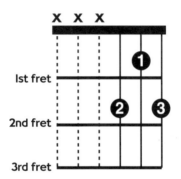

Three-String D⁷ Chord

Quarter Note

1 beat

Play E

1st string, open

Play F

1st string, 1st fret

Play G

1st string, 3rd fret

Play B

2nd string, open

Play C

2nd string, 1st fret

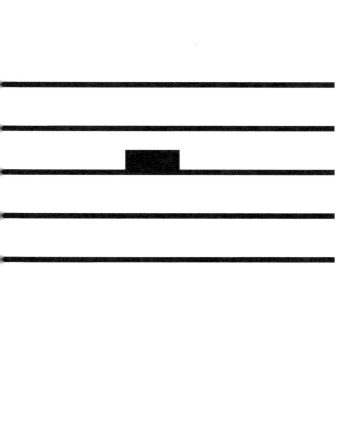

Half Rest

2 beats

Do not play for two beats.

Play D

2nd string, 3rd fret

Half Note

2 beats

Play G

3rd string, open

Play A

3rd string, 2nd fret

Whole Note

4 beats

Play D

4th string, open

Half-Note Slash

2 beats
Hold strum for two beats.

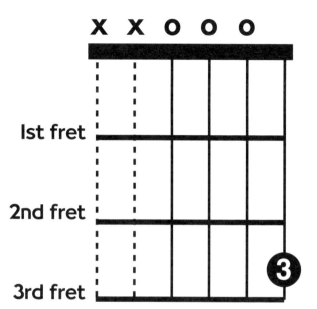

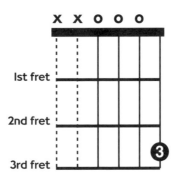

Four-String G Chord

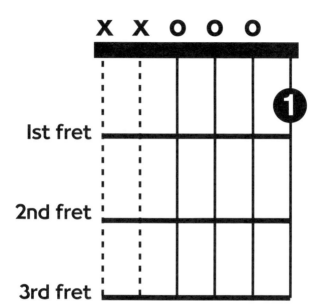

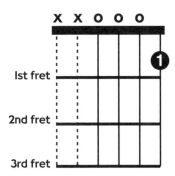

Four-String G⁷ Chord

Play E

4th string, 2nd fret

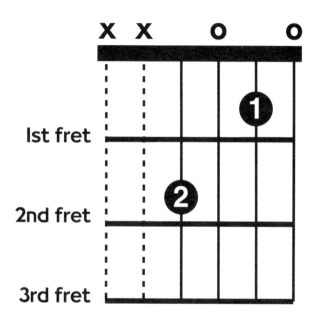

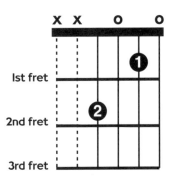

Four-String C Chord

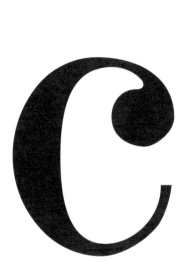

Time Signature:
Common Time

The same as $\frac{4}{4}$ time.

Play F

4th string, 3rd fret

$$\frac{3}{4}$$

Time Signature:
Three-Four Time

3 equal beats in every measure.

Dotted Half Note

3 beats

Play A

5th string, open

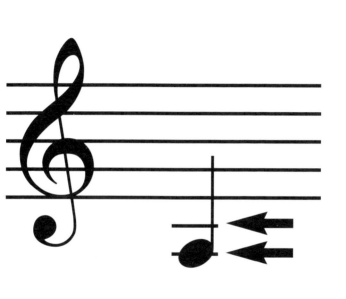

Ledger Lines

Extend the staff up or down.

Play B

5th string, 2nd fret

Play C

5th string, 3rd fret

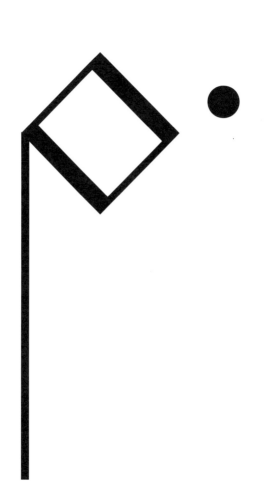

Dotted-Half-Note Slash

3 beats
Hold strum for three beats.

Play E

6th string, open

Play F

6th string, 1st fret

Fermata

Play the note longer than normal.
(Hold about twice as long.)

Play G

6th string, 3rd fret

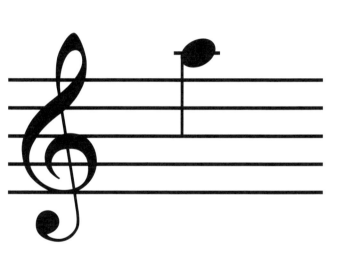

Play High A

1st string, 5th fret

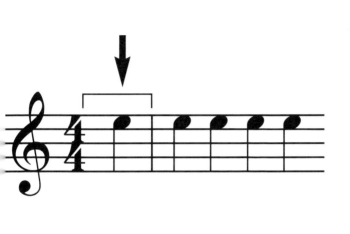

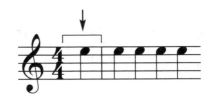

Pickup Measure

Just part of a measure that
begins a piece of music.

Andante

Andante

"ahn-DAHN-teh"

Tempo Sign:

Slow

Moderato

"moh-deh-RAH-toh"

Tempo Sign:

Moderately

Allegro

4

Allegro

"ah-LAY-groh"

Tempo Sign:

Fast

Play Three-String C Chord

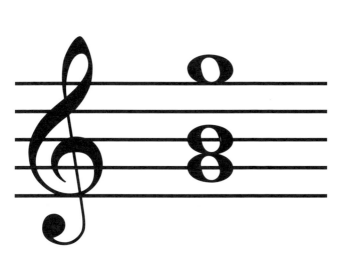

Play Three-String G Chord

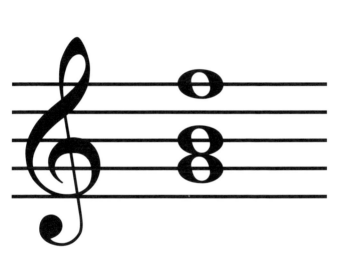

Play Three-String G⁷ Chord

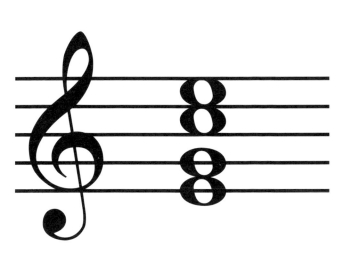

Play Four-String C Chord

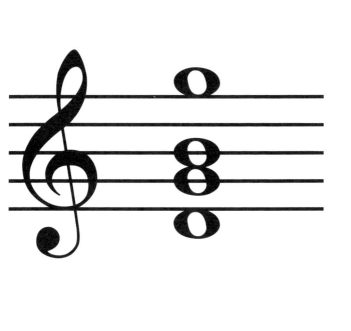

Play Four-String G Chord

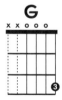

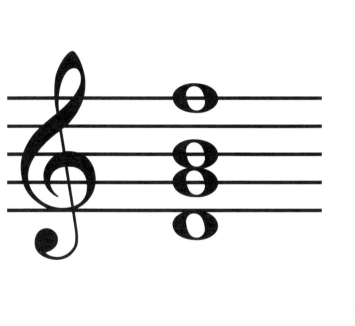

Play Four-String G⁷ Chord

Bass-Chord-Chord-Chord
Accompaniment

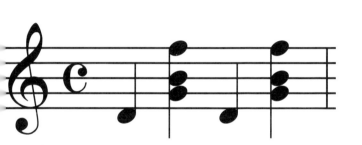

Bass-Chord-Bass-Chord
Accompaniment

Dynamic:
Piano
"PYAH-noh"

Soft

Dynamic:
Mezzo-Forte
"MED-zoh FOHR-teh"

Moderately loud

Dynamic:
Forte
"FOHR-teh"

Loud

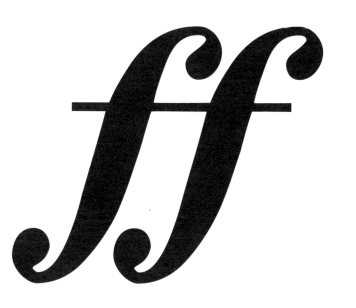

Dynamic:
Fortissimo

"fohr-TEE-see-moh"

Very loud

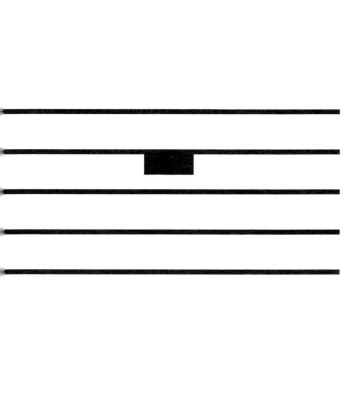

Whole Rest

Be silent for a whole measure.

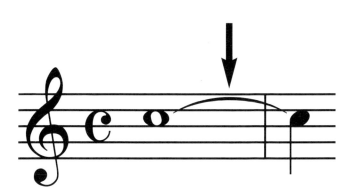

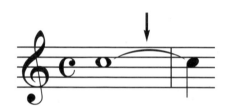

Tie

A curved line that connects two of the same note. Don't play the second note, but keep the first note playing.